All About Chutney

50 Delicious Chutney Recipes

By
BookSumo Press
All rights reserved

Published by
http://www.booksumo.com

ENJOY THE RECIPES?
KEEP ON COOKING WITH 6 MORE FREE COOKBOOKS!

Visit our website and simply enter your email address to join the club and receive your 6 cookbooks.

http://booksumo.com/magnet

https://www.instagram.com/booksumopress/

https://www.facebook.com/booksumo/

LEGAL NOTES

All Rights Reserved. No Part Of This Book May Be Reproduced Or Transmitted In Any Form Or By Any Means. Photocopying, Posting Online, And / Or Digital Copying Is Strictly Prohibited Unless Written Permission Is Granted By The Book's Publishing Company. Limited Use Of The Book's Text Is Permitted For Use In Reviews Written For The Public.

Table of Contents

5 . . . . .Mango & Raisin Chutney
6 . . . . .Tangy Fruit Chutney
7 . . . . .Plum-Ginger Chutney
8 . . . . .Pineapple & Cranberry Chutney
9 . . . . .Spiced Apple Chutney
10 . . . . . . .Loquat, Apple & Apricot Chutney
11 . . . . . . .Herbed Coconut Chutney
12 . . . . . . .Spiced Pear Chutney
13 . . . . . . .Hot Coconut & Chickpea Chutney
14 . . . . . . .Creamy Peanut Butter Chutney
15 . . . . . . .Spicy Date & Tamarind Chutney
16 . . . . . . .Sweet & Sour Chutney
17 . . . . . . .Hot Peach Chutney
18 . . . . . . .Autumn Chutney
19 . . . . . . .Spiced Dry Fruit Chutney
20 . . . . . . .Hot Pumpkin & Apple Chutney
21 . . . . . . .Apple, Pear & Tomato Chutney
22 . . . . . . .Creamy Coriander Chutney
23 . . . . . . .Apricot & Raisin Chutney
24 . . . . . . .Mango & Onion Chutney in Wine
25 . . . . . . .Citrus Apple Chutney
26 . . . . . . .Chili & Onion Chutney
27 . . . . . . .Slow Cooked Peach Chutney
28 . . . . . . .Lemony Chutney
29 . . . . . . .Mint & Almond Chutney
30 . . . . . . .Fruity Mustard Chutney
31 . . . . . . .Spiced Rhubarb & Currants Chutney
32 . . . . . . .Curried Apricot Chutney
33 . . . . . . .Apple & Cherry Chutney
34 . . . . . . .Apple & Sultana Chutney
35 . . . . . . .Persimmon & Apple Chutney
36 . . . . . . .Lemony Banana Chutney
37 . . . . . . .Coconut & Cilantro Chutney
38 . . . . . . .Lime & Sultanas Chutney
39 . . . . . . .Tamarillo & Raisins Chutney
40 . . . . . . .Spice Onion Chutney
41 . . . . . . .Spiced Veggie Chutney
42 . . . . . . .Spice Onion Chutney
43 . . . . . . .Fig & Apple Chutney
44 . . . . . . .Plum, Raisin & Onion Chutney
45 . . . . . . .Herbed Grape Chutney
46 . . . . . . .Minty Yogurt Chutney
47 . . . . . . .Mixed Veggie Chutney
48 . . . . . . .Sweet & Sour Chutney
49 . . . . . . .Caribbean Chutney
50 . . . . . . .Apple-Ginger Chutney
51 . . . . . . .Sweet & Spicy Apple Tomato Chutney
52 . . . . . . .Sweet Sour Onion Chutney
53 . . . . . . .Chutney with Raisins & Peanuts
54 . . . . . . .Cheesy Fruit Chutney Dip
55 . . . . . . .Chutney & Raisin Pilaf
56 . . . . . . .Creamy Chutney Coleslaw

Mango & Raisin Chutney

Prep Time: 20 mins
Total Time: 1 hr 5 mins

Servings per Recipe: 1
Calories   627.2
Fat   2.1g
Cholesterol   0.0mg
Sodium   3748.7mg
Carbohydrates   153.4g
Protein   4.2g

Ingredients

1 kg very firm mango
2 C. sugar
625 ml vinegar
1 (5 cm) pieces ginger, peeled
4 cloves garlic, peeled
2 - 4 tsps chili powder

4 tsps mustard seeds
8 tsps salt
1 C. raisins or 1 C. sultana

Directions

1. Peel the mango and then remove the pit and chop it.
2. In a pan, add sugar and vinegar, leaving about 20ml and simmer, stirring occasionally for about 10 minutes.
3. Meanwhile in a food processor, add remaining vinegar, garlic and ginger and pulse till a paste forms.
4. Transfer the paste into a pan and simmer, stirring continuously for about 10 minutes.
5. Stir in the mango and remaining ingredients and simmer, stirring occasionally for about 25 minutes or till desired thickness of chutney.
6. Transfer the chutney into hot sterilized jars and seal tightly and keep aside to cool.
7. This chutney can be stored in dark place for about 1 year but remember to refrigerate after opening.

TANGY FRUIT
Chutney

🍳 Prep Time: 25 mins
🕒 Total Time: 40 mins

Servings per Recipe: 1
Calories   456.6
Fat   5.7g
Cholesterol   0.0mg
Sodium   171.9mg
Carbohydrates   105.8g
Protein   2.5g

Ingredients

1 lb fresh cranberries
2 1/2 C. sugar
1 C. water
1/2 tsp salt
1/2 tsp ground cinnamon
1/2 tsp ground cloves
1 medium onion, chopped

1 medium tart apple, peeled and cubed
1 medium pear, peeled and cubed
1 C. raisins
1/4 C. lemon juice
1/2 C. chopped walnuts

Directions

1. In a large pan, add cranberries, water, sugar, spices and salt on medium-high heat and bring to a boil.
2. Reduce the heat to low and cook, stirring occasionally for about 10 minutes.
3. Stir in pear, apple and onion and cook for about 5 minutes.
4. Remove from heat and immediately, stir in lemon juice and raisins.
5. Transfer the chutney into a bowl and refrigerate for at least 8 hours.
6. While serving, fold in walnuts.
7. Enjoy with a dressing or meat of your choice.

Plum-Ginger Chutney

Prep Time: 20 mins
Total Time: 1 hr 10 mins

Servings per Recipe: 1
Calories   567.7
Fat   1.0g
Cholesterol   0.0mg
Sodium   1190.1mg
Carbohydrates   142.6g
Protein   2.4g

Ingredients

- 3 1/2 C. purple plums, seeds removed
- 1 C. brown sugar
- 1 C. sugar
- 3/4 C. cider vinegar
- 1 C. golden seedless raisins
- 2 tsps salt
- 1/3 C. chopped onion
- 1 clove garlic, minced
- 2 tsps mustard seeds
- 3 tbsps chopped crystallized ginger
- 3/4 tsp cayenne

Directions

1. In a large nonreactive pan, mix together vinegar and sugar and bring to a boil.
2. Cook, stirring continuously till sugar is dissolved completely.
3. Stir in the remaining ingredients and bring to a boil.
4. Reduce the heat to low and cook, stirring occasionally for about 40-50 minutes or till desired thickness of chutney.
5. Transfer the chutney into hot sterilized jars and seal tightly and keep aside to cool.
6. For better taste use after about 1 month.

PINEAPPLE & Cranberry Chutney

Prep Time: 5 mins
Total Time: 15 mins

Servings per Recipe: 1
Calories	148.5
Fat	0.1g
Cholesterol	0.0mg
Sodium	2.6mg
Carbohydrates	38.2g
Protein	0.8g

Ingredients

- 20 oz. canned crushed pineapple (with juice)
- 1/4 C. sugar
- 2 tbsps apple cider vinegar
- 1 tbsp corn syrup
- 2 tbsps candied ginger, minced
- 1/4 C. dried cranberries

Directions

1. Drain the juice from the pineapple can and transfer into a pan with vinegar and sugar and cook, stirring occasionally till mixture reduces to 1/2 C.
2. Stir in the remaining ingredients and immediately, remove from heat.
3. Transfer the chutney into a bowl and refrigerate to chill before serving.

Spiced Apple Chutney

Prep Time: 1 hr
Total Time: 2 hrs 15 mins

Servings per Recipe: 10
Calories   708.1
Fat   1.7g
Cholesterol   0.0mg
Sodium   514.7mg
Carbohydrates   177.1g
Protein   4.5g

Ingredients

- 2 quarts chopped cored, pared tart apples
- 2 lbs raisins
- 1 C. chopped onion
- 1 C. chopped sweet red pepper
- 4 C. brown sugar
- 3 tbsps mustard seeds
- 2 tbsps ground ginger
- 2 tsps ground allspice
- 2 tsps salt
- 2 hot red peppers
- 1 garlic clove, crushed
- 1 quart vinegar

Directions

1. In a pan, mix together all the ingredients and simmer, stirring occasionally for about 1 hour and 15 minutes or till desired thickness of chutney.
2. Transfer the chutney into hot sterilized jars and seal tightly and place in a large bowl of boiling water for about 10 minutes.
3. (If you like mild flavored chutney than you can add 4 additional C. of apples).

LOQUAT, APPLE & Apricot Chutney

Prep Time: 1 hr
Total Time: 2 hrs 30 mins

Servings per Recipe: 120
Calories   28.9
Fat   0.1g
Cholesterol   0.0mg
Sodium   39.5mg
Carbohydrates   7.0g
Protein   0.1g

Ingredients

650 g loquats
4 large apples
300 g dried apricots
80 g gingerroot
4 tbsps mustard seeds
500 g raw sugar

750 ml cider vinegar
2 tsps salt
2 tsps crushed chilies

Directions

1. Peel, core and then chop the apple.
2. Cut the flower ends and stems of the loquat and remove the stones.
3. Slice the apricots thinly.
4. Julienned the ginger.
5. Crush the mustard seed.
6. In a pan, add all the ingredients and bring to a boil.
7. Reduce the heat and simmer, stirring occasionally for about 1 hour and 30 minutes or till the desired thickness of chutney.
8. Transfer the chutney into hot sterilized jars and seal tightly and keep aside to cool.
9. This chutney can be stored in a dark place for about 9 months but remember to refrigerate after opening.

Herbed Coconut Chutney

Prep Time: 10 mins
Total Time: 20 mins

Servings per Recipe: 8
Calories   16.1
Fat   0.5g
Cholesterol   0.0mg
Sodium   9.4mg
Carbohydrates   2.8g
Protein   0.6g

Ingredients

2 C. chopped fresh cilantro
1 C. chopped mint
1 tbsp fresh ginger, chopped
1 tbsp garlic, chopped
1 tbsp green chili, chopped

2 tbsps desiccated coconut
salt
1/4 C. lemon juice

Directions

1. In a grinder, add all the ingredients and a little water and grind till smooth.

SPICED PEAR
Chutney

🥘 Prep Time: 10 mins
🕐 Total Time: 1 hr 10 mins

Servings per Recipe: 20
Calories 156.5
Fat 0.2g
Cholesterol 0.0mg
Sodium 242.0mg
Carbohydrates 39.5g
Protein 0.6g

Ingredients

3 lbs pears, unpeeled, cored, diced
1 lb brown sugar
2 C. cider vinegar
1 onion, medium, chopped
1 C. golden raisin
1/4 C. preserved gingerroot, diced
1 garlic clove, minced

1/2 tsp cayenne pepper
2 tsps salt
1/2 tsp ground cinnamon
1/2 tsp ground cloves
2 tsps mustard seeds

Directions

1. In a large pan, mix together vinegar and brown sugar bring to a boil.
2. Stir in the remaining ingredients and reduce the heat to low.
3. Cook, stirring occasionally for about 1 hour or till desired thickness of chutney.
4. Transfer the chutney into hot sterilized jars and seal tightly and keep aside to cool or refrigerate, covered for about 3-4 weeks.
5. Enjoy as a side with lamb or eat with crackers and cream cheese as an appetizer.

Hot Coconut & Chickpea Chutney

Prep Time: 5 mins
Total Time: 10 mins

Servings per Recipe: 2
Calories   102.6
Fat   3.5g
Cholesterol   0.0mg
Sodium   8.4mg
Carbohydrates   15.0g
Protein   4.4g

Ingredients

1/2 large coconut, grated
2 tbsps bengal gram dal (split dried chickpeas) or 2 tbsps channa dal (dried chickpeas)
3 green chilies
3/4 C. water
1 tsp vegetable oil

1 tsp mustard seeds
1 tsp split Urad Dal (split black gram)
3 curry leaves

Directions

1. Heat 1/2 tsp of oil in a small frying pan and cook the chickpeas till golden brown.
2. Remove from heat and let them cool completely.
3. In a mixer, add chickpeas, green chilies, coconut and salt and pulse.
4. While the motor is running gradually, add the water and smooth everything then transfer it all into a bowl.
5. Heat the remaining oil in the same frying pan and cook the split black gram, mustard seeds and curry leaves till the seeds start to sputter.
6. Add the mustard seed mixture into the bowl with the chutney and stir to combine.

CREAMY
Peanut Butter Chutney

Prep Time: 5 mins
Total Time: 5 mins

Servings per Recipe: 1
Calories 44.8
Fat 3.2g
Cholesterol 0.0mg
Sodium 66.7mg
Carbohydrates 3.0g
Protein 1.7g

Ingredients

2 tbsps natural-style peanut butter
2 tbsps ketchup
1 garlic clove, minced
1/2 tsp cayenne pepper

Directions

1. In a bowl, add all the ingredients and about 4 tsps of water and stir till well combined.

Spicy Date & Tamarind Chutney

🥣 Prep Time: 5 mins
🕐 Total Time: 25 mins

Servings per Recipe: 1
Calories   408.6
Fat   0.2g
Cholesterol   0.0mg
Sodium   888.5mg
Carbohydrates   106.1g
Protein   1.2g

Ingredients

- 8 -10 large dates, pits removed
- 3/4 C. jaggery (Indian unrefined sugar) or 3/4 C. dark brown sugar
- 1 1/2 C. water
- 4 tbsps tamarind paste
- 1/4 tsp hot chili powder
- 1/2 tsp ground ginger
- 1 tsp ground garam masala
- 3/4 tsp salt

Directions

1. In a medium pan, mix together water, dates and jaggery or brown sugar and bring to a boil on medium heat.
2. Cook, stirring occasionally for about 7-8 minutes or till the dates become tender.
3. Stir in tamarind and immediately, remove from heat and let it cool slightly.
4. Transfer the date mixture into a blender and pulse till smooth.
5. Again, transfer the date mixture into a pan and bring to a gentle boil.
6. Simmer, stirring occasionally till desired thickness of chutney.
7. Stir in the spices and salt and remove from heat.
8. Transfer into an airtight container and preserve in the refrigerator.

SWEET & SOUR
Chutney

🥣 Prep Time: 5 mins
🕐 Total Time: 2 hrs 5 mins

Servings per Recipe: 1
Calories   656.4
Fat   4.5g
Cholesterol   0.0mg
Sodium   1431.5mg
Carbohydrates   149.6g
Protein   6.4g

Ingredients

1 head garlic, peeled, coarsely chopped
1 piece fresh ginger, about 2 inches long, 1 inch thick and 1 inch wide, peeled and coarsely chopped
1 1/2 C. red wine vinegar
1 (28 oz.) cans whole tomatoes
1 1/2 C. sugar
1 1/2 tsps salt
1/8-1/2 tsp cayenne pepper
2 tbsps golden raisins
2 tbsps blanched slivered almonds

Directions

1. In a blender, add ginger, garlic and 1/2 C. of vinegar and pulse till smooth.
2. In a heavy-bottomed pot, add the tomatoes with juice, sugar, remaining vinegar, cayenne pepper and salt and bring to a boil.
3. Stir in ginger puree and reduce the heat.
4. Simmer, stirring occasionally for about 1-1 1/2 hours or till desired thickness of chutney.
5. Stir in the raisins and almonds and simmer for about 5 minutes more.
6. Remove from heat and let it cool before serving.

Hot Peach Chutney

Prep Time: 10 mins
Total Time: 20 mins

Servings per Recipe: 6
Calories   45.9
Fat   0.3g
Cholesterol   0.0mg
Sodium   0.4mg
Carbohydrates   11.2g
Protein   0.9g

Ingredients

5 peaches, ripe
2 jalapenos, stems removed, diced
1 tbsp ginger, finely diced
1 tbsp sugar
1 tsp ground cinnamon
2 tsps lemon juice

Directions

1. Peel the peaches and then remove the pit and chop 3 of them in a bowl.
2. In a blender, add remaining peaches and pulse till a puree forms.
3. In a pan, mix together peach puree, ginger, jalapeños, sugar, lemon juice and cinnamon on medium heat.
4. Simmer, stirring occasionally for about 5-6 minutes.
5. Stir in the chopped peaches and simmer, stirring occasionally for about 3 minutes or till desired thickness of chutney.
6. Remove from heat and let it cool before serving.

AUTUMN
Chutney

Prep Time: 35 mins
Total Time: 1 hr 35 mins

Servings per Recipe: 1
Calories 513.5
Fat 1.0g
Cholesterol 0.0mg
Sodium 389.6mg
Carbohydrates 131.8g
Protein 4.8g

Ingredients

3/4 C. quartered pitted prune
3/4 C. quartered dried apricot
1 large onion, chopped
1 large tart apple, peeled and finely chopped
1/2 C. canned tomato, chopped drained seeded
1/3 C. granulated sugar
1/2 tsp ground ginger
1/4 tsp ground cinnamon
1/4 tsp clove
1/4 tsp nutmeg

1/4 tsp black pepper
1/4 tsp cayenne pepper
1/4 tsp salt
1/4 C. cider vinegar
1/4 tsp salt
1/4 C. cider vinegar

Directions

1. In a pan, mix together apricots, prunes and water and bring to a boil and immediately, remove from heat.
2. Cover the pan and keep aside for about 30 minutes.
3. Stir in the remaining ingredients and again bring to a gentle simmer on medium heat.
4. Reduce the heat to low and simmer, stirring occasionally for about 50-60 minutes or till desired thickness of chutney.
5. Transfer the chutney into sterilized jars and preserve.

Spiced Dry Fruit Chutney

Prep Time: 5 mins
Total Time: 35 mins

Servings per Recipe: 1
Calories	542.0
Fat	0.6g
Cholesterol	0.0mg
Sodium	614.7mg
Carbohydrates	138.1g
Protein	2.3g

Ingredients

- 1/2 C. water
- 3 medium apples, tart, diced
- 1 C. dried pitted prunes, diced
- 1 C. dried apricot, diced
- 1 C. cider vinegar
- 1 1/2 C. brown sugar, packed
- 1 tsp salt
- 1/2 tsp ground cinnamon
- 1/2 tsp black pepper
- 1/2 tsp ground cloves
- 1/2 tsp coriander
- 1/2 tsp curry powder
- 1/8 tsp crushed red pepper flakes
- 3 garlic cloves, mince.

Directions

1. In a large pan, add all the ingredients and bring to a boil and reduce the heat.
2. Simmer, stirring occasionally for about 20 minutes or till desired thickness of chutney.
3. Transfer the chutney into hot sterilized jars and seal tightly and keep aside to cool.

HOT PUMPKIN & Apple Chutney

🥣 Prep Time: 15 mins
🕐 Total Time: 1 hr 45 mins

Servings per Recipe: 1
Calories   492.1
Fat   2.1g
Cholesterol   0.0mg
Sodium   424.3mg
Carbohydrates   114.8g
Protein   4.0

Ingredients

2 1/2 lbs pumpkin flesh, in medium dice
1 1/2 lbs apples, peeled cored and diced
2 oz. fresh gingerroot, grated
3 fresh red chilies, chopped and seeded
4 tbsps mustard seeds

1 liter cider vinegar
1 lb light brown sugar
1 tsp salt

Directions

1. In a large pan, mix together all the ingredients except sugar and salt and bring to a boil and reduce the heat.
2. Simmer, stirring occasionally till the pumpkin is tender.
3. Stir in the sugar and salt and again bring to a boil and reduce the heat.
4. Simmer, stirring occasionally for about 1 hour or till the desired thickness of chutney.
5. Transfer the chutney into hot sterilized jars and seal tightly and keep aside to cool.
6. This chutney will be ready in 4 weeks to eat.
7. This chutney can be stored in dark place for about 2 years but remember to refrigerate after opening.

Apple, Pear & Tomato Chutney

Prep Time: 15 mins
Total Time: 1 hr 20 mins

Servings per Recipe: 1
Calories   1530.2
Fat   3.2g
Cholesterol   0.0mg
Sodium   2411.9mg
Carbohydrates   365.1g
Protein   11.9g

Ingredients

2 cooking apples, peeled, cored & grated
150 g onions, peeled & finely chopped
150 g golden sultana raisins
4 oranges, juice and zest of
300 g light brown sugar
1 tsp ground cinnamon
1 tsp freshly ground nutmeg
1 tsp cayenne pepper

3 pinches saffron strands
2 tsps salt
50 g fresh gingerroot, grated
300 ml white wine or 300 ml cider vinegar
750 g pears, peeled, cored and roughly chopped
350 g tomatoes, roughly chopped

Directions

1. In a large pan, mix together all the ingredients except tomatoes and pear and bring to a boil and reduce the heat.
2. Simmer, stirring occasionally for about 30-45 minutes or till the mixture becomes syrupy.
3. Stir in the tomatoes and pear and simmer, stirring occasionally for about 15-20 minutes or till desired thickness of chutney.
4. Transfer the chutney into hot sterilized jars and seal tightly and keep aside to cool.
5. This chutney will be ready in 4-8 weeks to eat.
6. This chutney can be stored in dark place for about 2 years but remember to refrigerate after opening

CREAMY CORIANDER
Chutney

Prep Time: 15 mins
Total Time: 15 mins

Servings per Recipe: 5
Calories 29.4
Fat 0.8g
Cholesterol 0.7mg
Sodium 256.9mg
Carbohydrates 4.7g
Protein 1.7g

Ingredients

200 g coriander leaves, roughly chopped
3 green chilies, roughly chopped
1 garlic clove, roughly chopped
1/2 tsp salt
1 tsp lemon juice
2 tsps tamarind juice
2 tsps coconut cream
2 - 3 tbsps natural yoghurt

Directions

1. In a blender, add 4-5 tbsps of water and all the ingredients except yogurt and pulse till a smooth paste forms.
2. Add the yogurt and pulse till well combined.
3. Transfer the chutney into an airtight container and refrigerate for up to 4 days.

Apricot & Raisin Chutney

Prep Time: 30 mins
Total Time: 1 hr 30 mins

Servings per Recipe: 12
Calories	288.9
Fat	0.7g
Cholesterol	0.0mg
Sodium	266.0mg
Carbohydrates	71.2g
Protein	2.6g

Ingredients

- 2 1/2 lbs apricots, pitted and quartered
- 1 lb brown onion, peeled and diced
- 2 C. sultana raisins
- 1 lb brown sugar
- 2 C. cider vinegar
- 1 tsp chili powder
- 2 tsps mustard seeds
- 1 1/4 tsps salt
- 1 tsp turmeric
- 3/4 tsp cinnamon

Directions

1. In a large pan, mix together all the ingredients except tomatoes and pear and bring to a boil and reduce the heat.
2. Simmer, stirring occasionally for about 1 hour or till desired thickness of chutney.
3. Transfer the chutney into hot sterilized jars and seal tightly and keep aside to cool.
4. You can serve this chutney immediately but for better taste use after some days.

MANGO & ONION
Chutney in Wine

🥣 Prep Time: 20 mins
🕐 Total Time: 1 hr 50 mins

Servings per Recipe: 1
Calories   612.4
Fat   1.0g
Cholesterol   0.0mg
Sodium   16.2mg
Carbohydrates   144.7g
Protein   3.0g

Ingredients

4 medium mangoes, peeled and coarsely chopped (1.7kg)
3/4 C. port wine
2 large white onions, chopped finely (400g)
1 C. coarsely chopped raisins (170g)
2 tsps grated fresh ginger
2 fresh Thai red chili peppers, chopped finely
2 C. sugar (440g)
3 C. malt vinegar
2 tsps yellow mustard seeds

Directions

1. In a large heavy-bottomed pan, add all the ingredients and simmer, stirring continuously till the sugar dissolves.
2. Simmer, stirring occasionally for about 90 minutes or till desired thickness of chutney.
3. Transfer the chutney into hot sterilized jars and seal tightly and keep aside to cool.
4. This chutney can be stored in dark place for about 6 months but remember to refrigerate after opening.

Citrus Apple Chutney

Prep Time: 10 mins
Total Time: 2 hrs 10 mins

Servings per Recipe: 1
Calories 542.2
Fat 1.3g
Cholesterol 0.0mg
Sodium 36.0mg
Carbohydrates 136.0g
Protein 5.3g

Ingredients

- 7 large oranges (preferably navels)
- 1 lemon
- 5 large granny smith apples
- 3 large onions, chopped
- 4 C. malt vinegar
- 1 1/2 C. dark brown sugar
- 3/4 C. golden raisin
- 1/4 C. fresh ginger, chopped
- 1 tbsp fresh ginger, chopped
- 6 large garlic cloves, minced
- 2 red bell peppers, seeded and chopped
- 2 green bell peppers, seeded and chopped
- 2 tbsps ground turmeric
- 1 1/2 tsps black pepper
- 1 tsp cayenne pepper
- 1 tsp crushed red pepper flakes

Directions

1. Grate the fresh peel of the lemon and oranges and remove the white pith completely.
2. Discard the seeds and then cut them into cubes.
3. Peel, core and chop the apple roughly.
4. In a large Dutch oven, add the fruit and all the remaining ingredients and bring to a boil on medium-high heat.
5. Reduce the heat to low and simmer, stirring occasionally for about 90 minutes.
6. Transfer the chutney into hot sterilized jars and seal tightly.
7. Place the jars into a large bowl of boiling water for at least 10 minutes.
8. This chutney can be stored in dark place for several months but remember to refrigerate after opening.

CHILI & ONION
Chutney

Prep Time: 10 mins
Total Time: 1 hr 10 mins

Servings per Recipe: 1
Calories	1442.3
Fat	1.1g
Cholesterol	0.0mg
Sodium	39.8mg
Carbohydrates	361.6g
Protein	10.0g

Ingredients

- 1 C. hot chili pepper
- 1 C. sugar
- 1 C. sultana
- 1 C. vinegar
- 1 C. onion

Directions

1. Chop the onion and chilies.
2. In a pan, mix together all the ingredients and bring to a boil.
3. Reduce the heat to low and simmer, stirring occasionally till desired thickness of chutney.
4. Transfer the chutney into hot sterilized jars and seal tightly and keep aside to cool.

Slow Cooked Peach Chutney

Prep Time: 10 mins
Total Time: 5 hrs 10 mins

Servings per Recipe: 1
Calories 453.7
Fat 1.0g
Cholesterol 0.0mg
Sodium 29.5mg
Carbohydrates 113.4g
Protein 4.5g

Ingredients

cooking spray
2 C. chopped onions
4 C. fresh peaches or 4 C. frozen peaches, peeled and sliced
1 C. golden raisin
1 C. light brown sugar
1/4 C. crystallized ginger
1 tsp mustard seeds
1/2 tsp ground ginger
1/4 tsp cinnamon
1/4 tsp ground cloves
1/4 C. flour
1/4 C. cider vinegar

Directions

1. Heat a lightly, greased skillet and sauté the onion till softened.
2. In a crockpot, add the onion and peaches, raisins, ginger, brown sugar and spices.
3. In a bowl, mix together vinegar and flour and add into crockpot and stir to combine.
4. Set the crockpot on low.
5. Cover and cook for about 5 hours.

LEMONY Chutney

🥣 Prep Time: 10 mins
🕐 Total Time: 30 mins

Servings per Recipe: 9
Calories   226.9
Fat   0.2g
Cholesterol   0.0mg
Sodium   20.3mg
Carbohydrates   57.7g
Protein   1.2g

Ingredients

1 1/2 C. brown sugar
2/3 C. apple cider vinegar
1/4 C. water
2 tbsps minced fresh ginger
3 tsps lemon zest
1 large cinnamon stick
4 C. fresh rhubarb, cut into about 1/2-inch pieces
1 1/2 C. dark raisins or 1 1/2 C. currants

Directions

1. In a pan, mix together all the ingredients except rhubarb and currants or raisins and bring to a boil and cook, stirring continuously till the sugar dissolves.
2. Reduce the heat to low and simmer, stirring occasionally for about 5 minutes.
3. Simmer remaining ingredients and bring to a boil on medium-high heat.
4. Reduce the heat to low and simmer, stirring occasionally for about 6-7 minutes.
5. Season with salt and black pepper and serve warm.
6. You can preserve this chutney in refrigerator.

Mint & Almond Chutney

Prep Time: 30 mins
Total Time: 30 mins

Servings per Recipe: 8
Calories 57.1
Fat 4.6g
Cholesterol 0.0mg
Sodium 2.6mg
Carbohydrates 2.6g
Protein 2.5g

Ingredients

1/2 C. raw peanuts, skins on
3 garlic cloves
1 chili
1/2 C. fresh mint leaves
2 tsps coriander seeds
1 tbsp vinegar
2 - 4 tbsps fresh lime juice, to taste
1 C. plain yogurt (optional)
salt
pepper

Directions

1. Set your oven to 350 degrees F before doing anything else.
2. In a baking sheet, place the peanuts and cook in oven for about 15 minutes or till toasted.
3. In a kitchen towel, wrap the peanuts and with your hands, and rub till the skin is removed.
4. In a food processor, add the almonds, mint, chili, garlic, coriander seeds and vinegar and pulse till well combined.
5. Transfer the mixture into a bowl and add the yogurt and lime juice and stir to combine.
6. Season with desired amount of salt and black pepper and refrigerate, covered.

FRUITY MUSTARD
Chutney

🥣 Prep Time: 10 mins
🕐 Total Time: 50 mins

Servings per Recipe: 18
Calories   60.1
Fat   0.2g
Cholesterol   0.0mg
Sodium   33.6mg
Carbohydrates   15.0g
Protein   0.4g

Ingredients

1 tbsp water
2 tsps mustard powder
1/2 C. sugar
1/2 C. cider vinegar
2 pears, peeled, cored, diced
1 mango, peeled, seeded, diced
1/3 C. dark seedless raisins
1 small onion, peeled and finely chopped
1 garlic clove, peeled and finely chopped
1/2 tsp ground ginger
1/4 tsp red pepper flakes, crushed
1/4 tsp salt

Directions

1. In a bowl, mix together mustard and water.
2. In a pan, mix together vinegar and sugar and bring to a boil, stirring continuously till the sugar dissolves.
3. Cook for about 10 minutes.
4. Stir in the mustard mixture and remaining all the ingredients and bring to a gentle simmer.
5. Simmer, stirring occasionally for about 30 minutes or till desired thickness of chutney.
6. Transfer into an airtight container and preserve in refrigerator for about 1 week.

Spiced Rhubarb & Currants Chutney

Prep Time: 10 mins
Total Time: 45 mins

Servings per Recipe: 16
Calories	69.5
Fat	0.0g
Cholesterol	0.0mg
Sodium	79.9mg
Carbohydrates	17.3g
Protein	0.4g

Ingredients

- 1 C. packed brown sugar
- 3 C. finely chopped rhubarb (about 1 lb)
- 1 C. finely chopped onion
- 1/2 C. cider vinegar
- 1/4 C. balsamic vinegar
- 1/4 C. dried currant
- 1 tbsp minced peeled fresh ginger
- 1 tsp paprika
- 1/2 tsp salt
- 1/8 tsp ground cardamom
- 1/2 jalapeno pepper, minced

Directions

1. In a pan, mix together all the ingredients and bring to a boil on medium-high heat.
2. Reduce the heat to low and simmer, stirring occasionally for about 35 minutes or till desired thickness of chutney.
3. This chutney can be served cold or warm as well.
4. You can preserve in refrigerator.

CURRIED APRICOT
Chutney

🥣 Prep Time: 15 mins
🕐 Total Time: 1 hr 15 mins

Servings per Recipe: 1
Calories	758.4
Fat	0.6g
Cholesterol	0.0mg
Sodium	38.8mg
Carbohydrates	195.7g
Protein	3.9g

Ingredients

- 1 medium onion, chopped
- 1 inch piece gingerroot, peeled and minced
- 2 C. drained canned apricots
- 1/2 C. white sugar or 1/2 C. brown sugar
- 1 C. apple cider or 1 C. rice wine vinegar
- 3 C. water
- 1 tsp curry powder
- 4 cardamom pods
- 2 inches cinnamon sticks
- minced chili pepper (optional)

Directions

1. In a pan, mix together all the ingredients and bring to a boil.
2. Reduce the heat to low and simmer, stirring occasionally for about 90 minutes or till desired thickness of chutney.

Apple & Cherry Chutney

Prep Time: 3 mins
Total Time: 13 mins

Servings per Recipe: 4
Calories   245.8
Fat   0.2g
Cholesterol   0.0mg
Sodium   595.7mg
Carbohydrates   61.3g
Protein   1.1g

Ingredients

- 1 (15 oz.) cans dark sweet cherries, drained
- 1 large tart apple, pared, cored, diced
- 3/4 C. vinegar
- 3/4 C. brown sugar, packed
- 1 tsp salt
- 1 tsp ground ginger
- 1 1/2 tsps fresh garlic, minced
- 1/4 tsp red chile, crushed

Directions

1. In a pan, mix together all the ingredients and bring to a boil.
2. Reduce the heat to low and simmer, stirring occasionally for about 20-30 minutes or till desired thickness of chutney.
3. This chutney can be served cold or warm as well and with all kinds of meat.

APPLE & SULTANA
Chutney

🥣 Prep Time: 15 mins
⏱ Total Time: 1 hr

Servings per Recipe: 1
Calories 447.9
Fat 0.7g
Cholesterol 0.0mg
Sodium 25.2mg
Carbohydrates 112.7g
Protein 2.4g

Ingredients

4 lbs tart apples
1 lb red onion
1/2 lb sultana or raisins
3/4 lb dark brown sugar
1 1/2 pints cider vinegar

2 tsps ground ginger
2 tsps ground cinnamon

Directions

1. In a large pan, mix together all the ingredients and cook till desired thickness of chutney.
2. Transfer the chutney into hot sterilized jars and seal tightly and preserve.

Persimmon & Apple Chutney

Prep Time: 10 mins
Total Time: 25 mins

Servings per Recipe: 1
Calories   366.0
Fat   12.1g
Cholesterol   30.5mg
Sodium   296.3mg
Carbohydrates   58.6g
Protein   2.2g

Ingredients

- 2 tbsps unsalted butter
- 2 bay leaves
- 2 cinnamon sticks
- 1/2 C. red onion
- 1 serrano pepper
- 1 fresh garlic clove
- 1/2 C. wine
- 4 persimmons
- 1 nectarine
- 1 apple
- 2 tbsps unbleached cane sugar
- 1 dash cayenne pepper
- 1/4 tsp cinnamon
- 2 tbsps lime
- 1/4 tsp fine sea salt

Directions

1. Melt butter in a pan and sauté the red onion, garlic, cinnamon sticks and bay leaves till the onion becomes tender.
2. Stir in the wine and cook till the liquid reduces to half.
3. Stir in the remaining ingredients and simmer, stirring occasionally for about 15 minutes or till desired thickness of chutney.
4. Remove from heat and discard bay leaves and cinnamon sticks.
5. You can season the chutney according to your liking.

LEMONY BANANA
Chutney

Prep Time: 10 mins
Total Time: 25 mins

Servings per Recipe: 1
Calories   145.4
Fat   0.6g
Cholesterol   0.0mg
Sodium   2.2mg
Carbohydrates   37.6g
Protein   1.8g

Ingredients

2 ripe bananas (1 1/2 C. mashed)
2 tbsps fresh lemon juice
2 pinches ground cloves
1 tsp freshly grated lemon rind

Directions

1. With a potato masher or fork, mash the banana slightly.
2. In a nonreactive bowl, add the mashed bananas and remaining ingredients and bring to a boil.
3. Simmer, stirring occasionally for about 15 minutes or till the desired thickness of chutney.
4. Transfer the chutney into hot sterilized jars and seal tightly and refrigerate for a couple of weeks.

Coconut & Cilantro Chutney

Prep Time: 15 mins
Total Time: 15 mins

Servings per Recipe: 1
Calories	464.4
Fat	44.1g
Cholesterol	0.0mg
Sodium	29.9mg
Carbohydrates	19.7g
Protein	5.2g

Ingredients

- 2 C. freshly grated coconut
- 1 C. chopped fresh cilantro leaves
- 3 tbsps lemon juice
- 1 tbsp minced fresh ginger
- 1 green chili peppers, such as serrano or 1 jalapeno, seeds and stem removed, minced
- salt

Directions

1. In a large bowl add all the ingredients and mix till well combined.
2. Cover and refrigerate for at least 1 hour.

LIME & SULTANAS
Chutney

🥣 Prep Time: 48 hrs
🕐 Total Time: 50 hrs

Servings per Recipe: 50
Calories 109.3
Fat 0.9g
Cholesterol 0.0mg
Sodium 286.4mg
Carbohydrates 26.6g
Protein 0.3 g

Ingredients

10 ripe yellowed limes
2 tbsps cooking salt
6 1/2 oz. raisins
5 oz. sultanas or raisins
3 tbsps peanut oil
2 tsps ground cumin
1 tsp ground coriander
1 tsp black mustard seeds

1/2 tsp chili powder
1/2 tsp ground black pepper
5 finely chopped garlic cloves
2 1/2 inches piece finely chopped gingerroot
1 1/4 C. malt vinegar
1 kg soft brown sugar

Directions

1. Cut each lime into 8 wedges and transfer into a large bowl and sprinkle with cooking salt.
2. With plastic wrap, cover the bowl and place it in a cool dark place for about 2 days, stirring occasionally.
3. Drain and rinse well and transfer into a food processor with raisins and sultanas and pulse it in batches till chopped finely.
4. In a large heavy-bottomed pan, add the ginger, garlic and spices and sauté for about 2-3 minutes.
5. Add the brown sugar, vinegar and lime mixture and bring to a boil, stirring continuously till the sugar dissolves.
6. Reduce the heat and simmer, stirring occasionally for about 90 minutes or till the desired thickness of chutney. Transfer the chutney into hot sterilized jars and seal tightly and keep aside to cool.
7. This chutney can be stored in dark place but remember to refrigerate after opening.

Tamarillo & Raisins Chutney

🥣 Prep Time: 20 mins
🕐 Total Time: 1 hr

Servings per Recipe: 1
Calories   555.6
Fat   4.7g
Cholesterol   0.0mg
Sodium   7.4mg
Carbohydrates 133.6g
Protein   1.7g

Ingredients

12 tamarillos
1 tbsp olive oil
1 onion, finely chopped
2 garlic cloves, crushed
1 long red chili, seeds removed, finely chopped
1 1/2 C. caster sugar
1 C. white wine vinegar

3/4 C. raisins
1 tsp allspice
1/2 tsp cinnamon

Directions

1. With a knife, make a small cross cut on the base of each tamarillo and place in a large bowl of boiling water and keep aside for about 10 minutes.
2. Drain well and then peel and chop roughly.
3. In a pan, heat oil on medium heat and sauté onion, chili and garlic for about 3 minutes or till tender.
4. Stir in the remaining ingredients and bring to a boil, stirring continuously.
5. Reduce the heat and simmer, stirring occasionally for about 20 - 25 minutes or till desired thickness of chutney.
6. Transfer the chutney into hot sterilized jars and seal tightly and keep aside to cool.

SPICE ONION
Chutney

🍲 Prep Time: 0 mins
🕐 Total Time: 10 mins

Servings per Recipe: 4
Calories 51.4
Fat 0.8g
Cholesterol 0.0mg
Sodium 551.8mg
Carbohydrates 10.6g
Protein 1.9g

Ingredients

1/2 tsp vegetable oil
1/2 C. tomato paste
1 tsp paprika
1/2 tsp ground cumin
1/4 tsp sugar
1/2 tsp salt
1/2 tsp garlic paste
1 C. red onion, chopped
cilantro

Directions

1. In a pan, heat oil and mix together tomato paste, garlic paste, sugar, cumin, paprika and salt.
2. Simmer, stirring occasionally for about 5 minutes
3. Remove from heat and let it cool.
4. Stir in the onion and serve with the garnishing of cilantro.

Spiced Veggie Chutney

Prep Time: 30 mins
Total Time: 1 hr 15 mins

Servings per Recipe: 1
Calories 597.6
Fat 1.4g
Cholesterol 0.0mg
Sodium 22.8mg
Carbohydrates 146.3g
Protein 4.8g

Ingredients

- 3 green peppers, cored, seeded and diced
- 3 red peppers, cored, seeded and diced
- 1 lb onion, skinned and roughly chopped
- 1 lb tomatoes, roughly diced
- 1 lb cooking apple, cored, peeled and chopped
- 3/4 lb demerara sugar or 3/4 lb brown sugar
- 2 tsps ground allspice
- 2 tsps nigella seeds, black onion seeds
- 1 tsp ground green peppercorn
- 1 tsp mustard seeds
- 3/4 pint malt vinegar

Directions

1. In a pan, mix together fruit, vegetables, sugar, spices and vinegar and bring to a boil on medium-high heat.
2. Reduce the heat and simmer, stirring occasionally till desired thickness of chutney.
3. Transfer the chutney into hot sterilized jars and seal tightly and keep aside to cool.
4. This chutney can be stored in dark place for about 1 year but remember to refrigerate after opening.

SPICE ONION
Chutney

🥣 Prep Time: 0 mins
🕐 Total Time: 10 mins

Servings per Recipe: 4
Calories 51.4
Fat 0.8g
Cholesterol 0.0mg
Sodium 551.8mg
Carbohydrates 10.6g
Protein 1.9g

Ingredients

1/2 tsp vegetable oil
1/2 C. tomato paste
1 tsp paprika
1/2 tsp ground cumin
1/4 tsp sugar
1/2 tsp salt
1/2 tsp garlic paste
1 C. red onion, chopped
cilantro

Directions

1. In a pan, heat oil and mix together tomato paste, garlic paste, sugar, cumin, paprika and salt.
2. Simmer, stirring occasionally for about 5 minutes
3. Remove from heat and let it cool.
4. Stir in the onion and serve with the garnishing of cilantro.

Fig & Apple Chutney

Prep Time: 20 mins
Total Time: 1 hr 20 mins

Servings per Recipe: 1
Calories   949.7
Fat   1.5g
Cholesterol   0.0mg
Sodium   958.0mg
Carbohydrates   237.4g
Protein   4.8g

Ingredients

- 850 g fresh figs, chopped
- 400 g dried figs, chopped
- 3 large red onions, finely chopped
- 3 medium apples
- 40 g fresh gingerroot, cut into fine matchsticks
- 2 tsps ground allspice
- 1 pinch dried chili pepper flakes
- 2 tsps finely grated lemon zest
- 700 g demerara sugar
- 2 tsps salt
- 800 ml red wine vinegar
- 2 tsps fresh ground black pepper

Directions

1. In a large pan, mix together all the ingredients and bring to a boil then reduce the heat to low.
2. Cover and simmer, stirring occasionally for about 30 minutes.
3. Uncover and simmer, stirring occasionally for about 1 hour or till desired thickness of chutney.
4. Transfer the chutney into hot sterilized jars and seal tightly and keep aside to cool.
5. This chutney can be stored in dark place for about 1 year but remember to refrigerate after opening.

PLUM, RAISIN & Onion Chutney

🥣 Prep Time: 30 mins
🕐 Total Time: 1 hr 10 mins

Servings per Recipe: 1
Calories 733.9
Fat 2.4g
Cholesterol 0.9mg
Sodium 1324.1mg
Carbohydrates 179.3g
Protein 5.3g

Ingredients

- 3 C. yellow onions, chopped
- 3 C. red onions, chopped
- 8 C. fresh plums, 1/2-inch cubes
- 1 C. golden raisin
- 1/2 C. candied ginger, chopped
- 1 1/2 C. brown sugar, packed
- 1 1/2 C. granulated sugar
- 1 1/2 C. cider vinegar
- 3/4 C. hoisin sauce
- 1 tbsp mustard seeds
- 2 tsps salt

Directions

1. In a large pan, mix together all the ingredients and cover and bring to a boil.
2. Uncover and simmer, stirring occasionally for about 40 minutes or till desired thickness of chutney.
3. Transfer the chutney into hot sterilized jars and seal tightly and store in a dark place or preserve in a refrigerator.

Herbed Grape Chutney

Prep Time: 10 mins
Total Time: 20 mins

Servings per Recipe: 1
Calories	24.1
Fat	0.5g
Cholesterol	1.2mg
Sodium	4.0mg
Carbohydrates	5.1g
Protein	0.2g

Ingredients

- 4 C. red seedless grapes
- 1 tbsp butter
- 1/2 C. chopped red onion
- 1 tsp fresh rosemary, snipped
- 1/4 tsp dried oregano, crumbled
- 2 tbsps balsamic vinegar

Directions

1. Melt butter in a large skillet and sauté the onion for about 5 minutes.
2. Stir in the rosemary and oregano and sauté for about 1 minute.
3. Meanwhile in a food processor, add the grapes and pulse till chopped roughly.
4. Stir in the vinegar and chopped grapes and cook for about 1-2 minutes or till heated completely.

MINTY YOGURT
Chutney

Prep Time: 3 mins
Total Time: 18 mins

Servings per Recipe: 4
Calories   15.7
Fat   0.8g
Cholesterol   2.9mg
Sodium   305.3mg
Carbohydrates   1.3g
Protein   0.8g

Ingredients

6 tbsps plain yogurt
1/2 tsp salt
2 tsps dried mint
1/2 tsp chili powder

Directions

1. In a large bowl, mix together all the ingredients and mix till well combined.
2. Refrigerate to chill for at least 15 minutes before serving.

Mixed Veggie Chutney

Prep Time: 10 mins
Total Time: 10 mins

Servings per Recipe: 8
Calories	21.7
Fat	0.0g
Cholesterol	0.0mg
Sodium	2.2mg
Carbohydrates	4.7g
Protein	0.4g

Ingredients

- 1/2 C. white vinegar
- 1 tbsp sugar
- 1 small cucumber, chopped
- 1 small red bell pepper, chopped
- 1 tbsp of fresh mint, chopped
- 1 tbsp lime juice
- 1 small onion, quartered & thinly sliced

Directions

1. In a bowl, add sugar and vinegar and stir to combine.
2. Add the remaining ingredients and stir till well combined.
3. Serve warm or chill after refrigerating. (Before using, remove from refrigerator and keep aside to return to room temperature).

SWEET & SOUR
Chutney

🥣 Prep Time: 30 mins
🕒 Total Time: 2 hrs

Servings per Recipe: 1
Calories 1229.4
Fat 11.3g
Cholesterol 0.0mg
Sodium 1023.8mg
Carbohydrates 286.1g
Protein 11.4g

Ingredients

2 C. packed light brown sugar
1 C. white vinegar
2 1/2 lbs ripe yellow nectarines, peel on and cut into 1/2-inch dice
1 (8 oz.) cans crushed pineapple in juice (not heavy syrup)
1 C. golden raisin
3 fresh garlic cloves, minced
1 inch piece fresh gingerroot, peeled and finely grated

1 tsp salt
1/2 tsp ground cloves
1 tsp red chili pepper flakes
1/2 C. sliced almonds

Directions

1. In a large nonreactive pan, mix together vinegar and sugar on high heat.
2. Bring to a boil and cook, stirring occasionally for about 10 minutes.
3. Stir in the remaining ingredients except almonds and bring to a boil.
4. Reduce the heat to low and simmer, stirring occasionally for about 60-90 minutes or till desired thickness of chutney.
5. Remove from heat and immediately, fold in the almonds.
6. Transfer the chutney into hot sterilized jars and seal tightly and keep aside to cool.
7. This chutney can be stored in dark place for about 1 year but remember to refrigerate after opening.

Caribbean Chutney

Prep Time: 10 mins
Total Time: 1 hr 10 mins

Servings per Recipe: 1
Calories   724.8
Fat   2.1g
Cholesterol   0.0mg
Sodium   295.9mg
Carbohydrates   186.7g
Protein   5.8g

Ingredients

- 1 small fresh pineapple, peeled, cored and chopped
- 1 medium fresh papaya, seeded, peeled and chopped
- 1 tbsp gingerroot, minced
- 6 tbsps sugar
- 1 tbsp hot chili paste

Directions

1. In a medium pan, add all the ingredients except chili paste on medium heat and cook, stirring occasionally for about 1 hour or till desired consistency.
2. Remove from heat and immediately, fold in chili paste.

APPLE-GINGER
Chutney

Prep Time: 5 mins
Total Time: 25 mins

Servings per Recipe: 4
Calories   219.5
Fat   17.5g
Cholesterol   45.7mg
Sodium   139.1mg
Carbohydrates   17.2g
Protein   0.5g

Ingredients

3 oz. whole butter
2 apples, peeled and diced
1 tsp small diced gingerroot, peeled
1 oz. brown sugar
2 tsps chili powder
3 oz. tequila

12 oz. apple cider
salt
lime juice

Directions

1. Melt butter in a heavy sauté pan and cook ginger, apple and brown sugar for about 5 minutes.
2. Stir in the apple cider, tequila and chili powder and cook for about 15 minutes or till liquid is absorbed completely.
3. Stir in the desired amount of lime juice, salt and black pepper.

Sweet & Spicy Apple & Tomato Chutney

Prep Time: 5 mins
Total Time: 30 mins

Servings per Recipe: 6
Calories   50.2
Fat   0.3g
Cholesterol   0.0mg
Sodium   5.5mg
Carbohydrates   12.2g
Protein   0.9g

Ingredients

5 -6 plum tomatoes, cored, peeled and cut into eighths
1 medium sweet onion, cut into 1-inch pieces
1 tart apple, peeled, cored and cut into eighths
2 garlic cloves, minced
1 1/2 tbsps brown sugar
1 tbsp paprika
1 bay leaf
salt, to taste

Directions

1. In a large microwave safe bowl, add all the ingredients and microwave on high for about 20-25 minutes or till desired doneness of chutney.
2. This chutney can be enjoyed warm or at room temperature as well.

SWEET & SOUR
Caramelized Onion Chutney

Prep Time: 15 mins
Total Time: 1 hr 10 mins

Servings per Recipe: 1
Calories 373.2
Fat 5.9g
Cholesterol 0.0mg
Sodium 35.1mg
Carbohydrates 76.8g
Protein 2.9g

Ingredients

8 red onions
1 red chili, de-seeded
2 bay leaves
25 ml olive oil
200 g brown sugar
2 tsps mustard seeds
150 ml balsamic vinegar
150 ml red wine vinegar

Directions

1. Cut the chili and onion into thin slices and then half the onion slices once more.
2. In a pan, mix together onion, chili, bay leaves and oil on low heat and simmer, stirring occasionally for about 20 minutes or till the onion slices become sticky and dark,
3. Stir in the remaining ingredients and simmer, stirring occasionally for about 30 minutes or till the chutney becomes dark and thick.
4. Transfer the chutney into hot sterilized jars and seal tightly and keep aside to cool.
5. For better taste use this chutney after about 1 month.

Chutney with Creamy Raisins & Peanuts

Prep Time: 15 mins
Total Time: 15 mins

Servings per Recipe: 1
Calories	854.5
Fat	68.2g
Cholesterol	124.7mg
Sodium	806.3mg
Carbohydrates	47.6g
Protein	24.0g

Ingredients

- 8 oz. cream cheese, softened
- 1/2 C. chopped green onion
- 1/2 C. golden raisin
- 1/2 C. chopped dry roasted peanuts
- 2 tsps curry powder
- 1 tsp ginger
- 1/2 C. prepared chutney, any flavor

Directions

1. In a large bowl, add all the ingredients except chutney and mix till well combined.
2. Divide the cheese mixture between serving bowls and place the chutney on top evenly.
3. Enjoy with the crackers of your choice.

CHEESY FRUIT
Chutney Dip

Prep Time: 5 mins
Total Time: 5 mins

Servings per Recipe: 1
Calories 437.8
Fat 43.3g
Cholesterol 137.7mg
Sodium 404.2mg
Carbohydrates 6.9g
Protein 7.9g

Ingredients

250 g cream cheese
250 g jar rosella fruit chutney
1 tbsp paprika
chili powder

Directions

1. In a large bowl, add all the ingredients and with an electric hand mixer, combine well.
2. Serve with fresh julienned veggies and corn chips.

Chutney & Raisin Pilaf

Prep Time: 10 mins
Total Time: 35 mins

Servings per Recipe: 4
Calories 323.9
Fat 8.0g
Cholesterol 0.0mg
Sodium 434.0mg
Carbohydrates 54.7g
Protein 9.5g

Ingredients

- 1 C. long grain rice
- 2 1/4 C. chicken broth, lower sodium
- 1/2 C. chutney
- 1/2 C. golden raisin
- 1/2 tsp curry powder
- 1/2 C. slivered almonds, toasted in oven

Directions

1. In a pan, add the broth and bring to a boil on medium heat and slowly, stir in the rice. (Adding everything slowly will prevent a quick boil)
2. Reduce the heat to low and simmer, covered for about 20 minutes.
3. Remove from heat and immediately, stir in the chutney, curry powder, and raisins.
4. Keep aside, covered for at least 5 minutes for the flavors to mix well.
5. Serve with a garnishing of almonds.

CREAMY CHUTNEY
Coleslaw

Prep Time: 5 mins
Total Time: 5 mins

Servings per Recipe: 6
Calories 130.8
Fat 10.6g
Cholesterol 13.5mg
Sodium 156.8mg
Carbohydrates 8.7g
Protein 1.4g

Ingredients

1 (8 oz.) jars chutney
1/2 C. mayonnaise
1/2 C. sour cream
1/4 C. fresh cilantro, chopped
2 tsps lime juice

1 (8 oz.) bags coleslaw mix
1/2 red onions or 1/2 onion, of choice

Directions

1. In a bowl, all the ingredients except the coleslaw and onion and beat till well combined.
2. In another large bowl, mix together coleslaw and onion. Add chutney mixture and toss to coat well.
3. Before serving, refrigerate for at least 1 hour.

ENJOY THE RECIPES?
KEEP ON COOKING WITH 6 MORE FREE COOKBOOKS!

Visit our website and simply enter your email address to join the club and receive your 6 cookbooks.

http://booksumo.com/magnet

https://www.instagram.com/booksumopress/

https://www.facebook.com/booksumo/